EVIL PRESENCE

TOTAL DESTRUCTION OF DEMONIC POSSESSION & OPPRESSION IN HOMES, BODY ORGANS, OFFICES & PROPERTIES. ENOUGH IS ENOUGH

Prayer M. Madueke

PRAYER
PUBLICATIONS
UNITED STATES

MESSAGE FROM THE AUTHOR

PRAYER M. MADUEKE
CHRISTIAN AUTHOR

My name is Prayer Madueke, a spiritual warrior in the Lord's vineyard, an accomplished author, speaker, and expert on spiritual warfare and deliverance. I have published well over 100 books on every area of successful Christian living. I am an acclaimed family and relationship counselor with several titles dealing with critical areas in the lives of the children of God. I travel to several countries each year speaking and conducting deliverance sessions, breaking the yokes of demonic oppression and setting captives free.

It would be a delight to collaborate with you or your ministry in organized crusades, ceremonies, marriages and marriage seminars, special events, church ministration and fellowship for the advancement of God's kingdom here on earth.

You can find all my books on my webstore: store.madueke.com

Feel free to visit my website madueke.com for devotionals and other materials. God bless you.

TABLE OF CONTENTS

ONE

GHOST IN OUR MIDST

T he reality of demonic presence, ghosts in our midst, dark angels living with us which kept not their first estate, but left their own habitation to establish their second estate, homes here on this earth is getting visibly out every day. Many people, especially in developed world who were in doubts of these activities, the operations and the presence of this demons are visibly experiencing their attacks. It is a biblical fact that some angelic creature, demons who were created by God, housed by God in heaven rebelled against Him and was cast out to the earth where they live now to cause trouble against humanity.

> And the angels which kept not their first estate,
> but left their own habitation, he hath reserved
> in everlasting chains under darkness unto the
> judgment of the great day. Likewise, also these

filthy dreamers defile the flesh, despise dominion, and speak evil of dignities.

— JUDE 6, 8

But while men slept, his enemy came and sowed tares among the wheat, and went his way.

— MATTHEW 13:25

In the early pasts, they appear to people mostly in their dreams with the purpose of defiling, polluting, corrupting their bodies to destroy God's image and his likeness. That was what these demonic spirits achieved in the lives of people living in the ancient cities of Sodom and Gomorrah. Immediately this was achieved, the inhabitant of the two cities lost divine image, God's likeness and nature. Thereafter, they began to give themselves to fornication, going after strange flesh, despising dominions to speak evil of dignities.

Even as Sodom and Gomorrah, and the cities about them in like manner, giving themselves over to fornication, and going after strange flesh, are set forth for an example, suffering the vengeance of eternal fire.

— JUDE 1:7

And the Lord said, Because the cry of Sodom
and Gomorrah is great, and because their sin is
very grievous.

— GENESIS 18:20

These demonic spirits went about from person to person, place
to place, house to house without regards, respects to people's
titles, honor, position and securities placed in places. Human
built gates, doors, roadblocks, weapons and security personnel
are nothing to them. You may exercise dominion over other
creature, create boundary and restrictions to people under you
but these evil personalities despise such dominion. You may
have a supreme authority, sovereignty and give orders to
human beings under you and they obey but not these wicked
spirits. Their aim is to dominate, act superior, influence evil
actions everywhere, force people to do what they want, take the
uppermost position, control or live in preeminence, rule and
reign over other creatures here on earth. They want to take the
highest rank, or jurisdiction to issue orders, to exert the
supreme determining, guiding influence, to occupy
everywhere, be more elevated and superior in position than
other creatures in earth. So, no matter your rank, position as a

woman, man, professor, manager, president, bishop, pope, weak, strong or army general; these spirits despise it. Not only that, the speak evil of your quality, honor, esteem, office, legal title of nobility or state of being worthy. The question is how did these fallen angels, demons, principalities, evil powers, rulers of darkness of this world and spiritual wickedness in the high places achieve the above?

> Now the serpent was more subtill than any beast of the field which the Lord God had made. And he said unto the woman, Yea, hath God said, Ye shall not eat of every tree of the garden? And the woman said unto the serpent, we may eat of the fruit of the trees of the garden: But of the fruit of the tree which is in the midst of the garden, God hath said, Ye shall not eat of it, neither shall ye touch it, lest ye die.
>
> — GENESIS 3:1-3

Among the creatures, man was the only creature God created in his likeness, image to dominate, rule, reign over another creature as a god. From the beginning, Satan, evil spirits and all fallen angel have no power to rule or reign over other creature. He stole that power and right to rule and reign when Eve in the garden listened to his lies, looked at and admired the forbidden fruit, doubted God, desired what God forbidden, took the forbidden fruit and tempted Adam to do likewise.

> And the serpent said unto the woman, Ye shall
> not surely die: For God doth know that in the
> day ye eat thereof, then your eyes shall be
> opened, and ye shall be as gods, knowing good
> and evil. And when the woman saw that the tree
> was good for food, and that it was pleasant to
> the eyes, and a tree to be desired to make one
> wise, she took of the fruit thereof, and did eat,
> and gave also unto her husband with her; and
> he did eat.
>
> — GENESIS 3:4-6

Right from the day Adam and Eve cooperated with the devil and handed over their rights, position, rank and dominion over every creature, everyone that are born here on earth became a slave to the devil and inherited powers to sin and to become sinners. The first work that the devil did was to defile the mind and his conscience, enslave the will, darken his understanding, corrupt his moral nature and became a dominating tyrant against everyone born in this earth (Titus 1:15; Romans 7:18;

Ephesians 4:18; Romans 8:7-20). He became the worse enemy of man, if not the only human adversary, father of lies, murderer, prince of this world, rulers of darkness, accuser, old serpent, sinner and many other bad names (1 Peter 5:8; John 8:44; John 14:30; Ephesians 6:12; Revelation 12:10, 11; 1 John 3:8). Therefore, everyone born here on earth inherited sin before committing sin to be a sinner. With the plantation of sin in the heart of man, he went ahead to destroy God's image, divine likeness and godly nature. He achieves the above by visiting man constantly in the dream to plant evil desires to do ungodly things, unrighteous things, unholy things, foolish things to dishonor their bodies between themselves. He succeeded in changing the truth of God into a lie like he deceived Eve in the garden. Man worshipped him, started serving him, bowing down to him, praying to God with an image and calling the names of dead people, saints in prayers than the creator (Romans 1:18-25).

> For this cause God gave them up unto vile affections: for even their women did change the natural use into that which is against nature: And likewise also the men, leaving the natural use of the woman, burned in their lust one toward another; men with men working that which is unseemly, and receiving in themselves

that recompence of their error which was meet.
Being filled with all unrighteousness,
fornication, wickedness, covetousness,
maliciousness; full of envy, murder, debate,
deceit, malignity; whisperers, Backbiters, haters
of God, despiteful, proud, boasters, inventors
of evil things, disobedient to parents, Without
understanding, covenant breakers, without
natural affection, implacable, unmerciful: Who
knowing the judgment of God, that they which
commit such things are worthy of death, not
only do the same, but have pleasure in them
that do them.

— ROMANS 1:26-27, 29-32

Though, from the beginning, all men knew the truth, the law makers, community leaders, city elders, nations and religious leaders knew what is right but because of the negative influence of the ghosts in our midst, they reject the truth they used to know. They once had revelation from heaven against doing ungodly things but they on their own chose to hold the truth in unrighteousness. They refused to glorify God as God but started thinking, imagining on what to gain in doing foolish things. That was how they began to gather, plan, form evil gangs and some brought stones together and called them gods. Others offered sacrifices to demons, dedicated their children, born and unborn to idols. Some worshipped images, spoke to some powers in the waters, swore to them, made many promises to evil spirits, looked up to them, walked after them and became their slaves. Let me tell you the simple truth, the worse sin that God hate most is idolatry. Please, if you want peace here in this world and after death, avoid idolatry, reject it, come out of it and serve the only true God, the creator of heaven and earth. Idolatry is an abomination to God, it is unprofitable and defiling, hateful to God, it is bloody and abominable; it is vain and foolish (Judges 10:14; Ezekiel 20:7; Deuteronomy 7:25; 16:25). Many people are confused, asking why am I eating in the dreams, having sex in the dreams with my husband, wife, unknown people, putting on old school uniform, writing exams that I wrote physically many years ago and passed? Some will be visiting their places of birth in their dreams, where they lived before, putting on old school uniforms and each time these dreams come they will encounter problems physically, failures, defeat, shame, disappointments and disgrace. Many will experience blockages at the edge of breakthroughs, make heart breaking painful and unpardonable mistakes. Inability to complete any good project or ventures but end in failure or in poor finishing. Some will be harassed by enemies, hated and rejected by people everywhere they go without good reasons and their good will always be turned against them for evil. Many will experience strange sickness, mysterious attacks in their bodies, in their offices and worse; at their homes. Victims are denied of their due promotions, rights, benefits, entitlements without reasons and they meet uncompromised enemies, witches and wizards wherever they run to. Others will make wrong choice in marriage, relationships, have problematic neighbors, experience periodical attacks, oppressions, failures, defeats and frustrations without reasons. They are never at rest, in joy, happiness or free from life's battle but always fighting battles with stubborn and long-time problem. They meet wrong people, enemies, people always misunderstand them, misinterpret them; they face shame, disgrace and reproach. Good doors, good things, good people avoid them to suffer and die alone without help. Through personal involvement with occultic churches, secrets societies, witchcraft groups, family contaminated background, occultic idolatrous parents, heathen ancestors, a spirit or more demons from their altars can marry you.

Thou shalt betroth a wife, and another man shall lie with her: thou shalt build a house, and thou shalt not dwell therein: thou shalt plant a vineyard, and shalt not gather the grapes thereof. So that the man that is tender among you, and very delicate, his eye shall be evil

toward his brother, and toward the wife of his
bosom, and toward the remnant of his children
which he shall leave.

— DEUTERONOMY 28:30, 54

At that point, they will be visiting you in the dreams and if they have sex with your parent at your conception, you will be defiled, polluted and contaminated to behave like them from early stage. In other to waste some of their victims early in life, they will close your dream life to prevent you from knowing what goes on in your life through dreams. To some, they will cause you to ignore your dreams until it is almost too late to fight. Many people see themselves caring pregnancy, breast feeding, nursing babies and doing all manner of things in their dreams and yet they are manipulated to ignore them. Some die young, grow up to gather but will not enjoy the fruits of their labor, while others give birth to unprofitable children, captured early by these spirits and taken to captivity.

Thy sons and thy daughters shall be given unto
another people, and thine eyes shall look, and
fail with longing for them all the day long: and
there shall be no might in thine hand. Thou shalt

> beget sons and daughters, but thou shalt not
> enjoy them; for they shall go into captivity.
>
> — DEUTERONOMY 28:32, 41

Therefore, most people are wedded to these spirits unknown to them, doors of greatness are closed against their business, efforts in life and they became failures and defeated in life. Some are prevented not to marry at all, others marry very late and when they finally get married, they marry an enemy. At that point, their marriage, relationships bring pains, agony, endless battles, demonic challenges, regrets, unprofitable labors, childlessness, birth to strange children, hatred, sexual imbalance, cheating, troubles, fighting, terminal sickness, separation, multiple remarrying and divorcing. They are bewitched to have wrong desires, sexual abominations with opposite sex, engage in crimes, rebellion, violence, endless battles of life, suffering, hardship and lack in the midst of plenty. Even as a Christian, if you don't know how to handle it, go into warfare, they will never allow you to enjoy your Christian life

> Submit yourselves therefore to God. Resist the
> devil, and he will flee from you.
>
> — JAMES 4:7

> Finally, my brethren, be strong in the Lord, and
> in the power of his might. Put on the whole
> armour of God, that ye may be able to stand
> against the wiles of the devil. For we wrestle not
> against flesh and blood, but against
> principalities, against powers, against the rulers
> of the darkness of this world, against spiritual
> wickedness in high places.

— EPHESIANS 6:10-12

They will fight you as a Christian and make sure you don't pursuer any good venture to a successful end or without a deadly mortal battle. Some experience ups and downs in everything they do without finishing well. Some are wedded to extreme bad character that force itself into your life once in a while or at a particular season; examples, excessive anger, irritations at a slightest offence or even when no one offends them. Some Christians are unnecessary proud, pompous, filled with lusts and uncontrollable desires for immorality and they end up every year without achieving any meaningful thing. The activities of ghost in our midst are endless, uncountable because they are responsibly to all abominations here on earth that leads to failures, defeats and all manner of suffering.

And upon her forehead was a name written,
Mystery, Babylon the Great, the Mother of
harlots and abominations of the earth. And he
saith unto me, the waters which thou sawest,
where the whore sitteth, are peoples, and
multitudes, and nations, and tongues.

— REVELATION 17:5, 15

Through some of these principalities, powers, depending on
where you are born, living, your language, tongues or nation;
they sit upon your destiny. They sit upon people's marriages,
health, job, finances, wealth, silver, gold, your children, rights,
benefits and entitlements. Unless you fight, you may remain
and die in their bondage even as a true child of God who live in
ignorance of how to be delivered.

TWO

PEOPLE IN DOUBLE BONDAGE

In the time of Jeremiah, there are people who were forbidden from getting married even with their good certificate, exposure, beauty and endowed greatness. The word of God through Jeremiah forbids and warned believers not to get married to them, no matter their reasons. The reason is because people born in the place, family, their mothers and fathers are polluted, contaminated and defiled by the gods of the land. The gods of the land by the means of evil covenant with its inhabitants are possessed with grievous deaths demons.

> The word of the Lord came also unto me,
> saying, thou shalt not take thee a wife, neither
> shalt thou have sons or daughters in this place.
> For thus saith the Lord concerning the sons and

concerning the daughters that are born in this place, and concerning their mothers that bare them, and concerning their fathers that begat them in this land; They shall die of grievous deaths; they shall not be lamented; neither shall they be buried; but they shall be as dung upon the face of the earth: and they shall be consumed by the sword, and by famine; and their carcases shall be meat for the fowls of heaven, and for the beasts of the earth.

— JEREMIAH 16:1-4

The deaths spirit living inside such people are not ordinary spirit of deaths that are common in other places. This kind of deaths doesn't kill people immediately to be buried but will leave them alive to walk and live here on earth as walking corpses. It means that the demons of grievous deaths inside of them at a certain age or after a level of achievement, marriage or when they are about to be celebrated starts killing. When the spirits start killing, no one can help, pity, save, deliver or render any assistance. Those who will try to pray, help or pity such people will be attacked by the same spirit and if such helpers refuse to run away, withdraw their helps and run for their own lives, they will suffer the same fate. Ministers of the gospel, compassionate deliverance and weeping prophets may pray, fast and try to assist but God will refuse to answer.

> And I will cast you out of my sight, as I have cast out all your brethren, even the whole seed of Ephraim. Therefore, pray not thou for this people, neither lift up cry nor prayer for them, neither make intercession to me: for I will not hear thee.
>
> — JEREMIAH 7:15-16

Once their judgment, problems starts, all that gives them joy, peace, happiness, respect, honor will begin to die one after the other in mysterious ways. To some, it could be their relationship with others that will die first, health, business, marriage, finances, job, helpers or the source of their greatness. These grievous deaths start in different ways, forms; depending on the person involve, where he or she is born, their ancestors and the type of demons that are involved. Everybody that meets them, including medical doctors, witch doctors, loved ones, ministers, family members, things that makes life easy, drugs and every creature here on earth will not be able to render help. People, every other creature will see them and treats them as dungs upon the face of the earth and will hate them, attack them and reject them without reasons. Every destructive weapon, harmful objects, swords, famine of good things will fight them until they are consumed. All the good things attached to their wealth, food vitamins, God's presence, mercy and grace will abandon what they have until they will be reduced to carcasses and feasts to the fowls of heaven, and the beasts of the earth. When people in this category will face the above fate, sufferings, hardships, problems, troubles without help, they will begin to ask why and God will answer?

> And it shall come to pass, when thou shalt shew this people all these words, and they shall say unto thee, wherefore hath the Lord pronounced all this great evil against us? or what is our iniquity? or what is our sin that we have committed against the Lord our God? Then shalt thou say unto them, Because your fathers have forsaken me, saith the Lord, and have walked after other gods, and have served them, and have worshipped them, and have forsaken me, and have not kept my law; And ye have done worse than your fathers; for, behold, ye walk everyone after the imagination of his evil heart, that they may not hearken unto me.
>
> — JEREMIAH 16:10-12

The first bondage is inherited sin with the problems associated to such types of sins while the second bondage is sins you actually committed with problems associated to them. If anyone in your lineage, family or parents ever committed sin, walked after other gods, forsook God in the past, you are a victim of evil inheritance. If they have served other gods, worshipped them, bowed down to images, swore to other gods or broke God's commandments, you are a victim of evil inheritance. If you are doing the same thing, under the bondage of family bondage, sinful lifestyle, sinful character, you are a victim of double bondage and are bound to suffer double. Checking from the past generations, our present generation has done worse than the past generations put together. That is why evil, problems and impossibilities has increased and that is why many are suffering without help. That is why many are dead under grievous deaths without help, living without life, seen as dung upon the earth, being rejected and hated. That is why many are being consumed in mass death, wars, battles and demonic spirits are feasting on living souls as carcasses. That is why many in their residences are experiencing the presence of ghosts and are possessed by demonic spirits. That is why many are not married, having no peace and the married have inexplicable crises, fighting, childlessness, abortions, separations, divorce and famine of every good things. That is why there is no peace, true helpers, wars, mass deaths, mass burial, many woes, lies, robberies, evil noises, incurable demonic whips, movements of war weapons, dangerous spears (Nahum 3:1-3). Believers who because of temporary hardship, famine, temptation, satanic attack enter cult, seek for help wrongly, deny God, break his covenant and enter into covenant with any of the fallen angels will suffer more. They may get a temporary prosperity, supply of every need but will not enjoy their corrupt wealth.

> Then all the men which knew that their wives had burned incense unto other gods, and all the women that stood by, a great multitude, even all the people that dwelt in the land of Egypt, in Pathros, answered Jeremiah, saying, As for the word that thou hast spoken unto us in the name of the Lord, we will not hearken unto thee. But we will certainly do whatsoever thing goeth forth out of our own mouth, to burn incense unto the queen of heaven, and to pour out drink offerings unto her, as we have done, we, and our fathers, our kings, and our princes, in the cities of Judah, and in the streets of Jerusalem: for then had we plenty of victuals, and were well, and saw no evil. But since we left off to

> burn incense to the queen of heaven, and to
> pour out drink offerings unto her, we have
> wanted all things, and have been consumed by
> the sword and by the famine.

> — JEREMIAH 44:15-18

If you enter into covenant with evil spirit, fallen angels who counterfeit themselves as angels of light, departed saints, you will suffer more. Unless you break the inherited covenant, your personal sins, no matter who prays for you, God will not answer. Once you accept any false doctrine, pray and ask your dead father to help you, pray through any dead saint or ask them to pray for you when you know that they are not omnipresent, you will be cast out from God's sight. Once you are deceived to pray, using the name of someone who is dead, who can no longer hear, be physically consult, any dead person through sacrifice, worship, you became a traitor before God (Exodus 32:33; Hebrews 3:19; 4:1; 10:38, 39; 1 Timothy 4:1, 2; Ezekiel 3:20; John 15:2, 6; Luke 9:62; 11:24-26). Once you deviate from the word of God, you become an outcast, a captive, a leper before God and everything will turn against you.

> Beware lest any man spoil you through
> philosophy and vain deceit, after the tradition

of men, after the rudiments of the world, and
not after Christ.

— COLOSSIANS 2:8

Once you backslide, walk after other gods, God will forsake you, Satan, all evil spirit will attack you and your name will be removed from the book of life. Once you decide to continue in sin, the wrath of God will come upon you, you will be spiritually dead, exposed to demonic attacks, shame, reproach, disgrace, incurable diseases and finally; eternal death. If you are presently under satanic attack and wish to come out completely the only way out is repentance, forsaken of all sins, restitution and consecration to God to do his will. You must renounce human philosophy, tradition of men, your church doctrine that contradicts God's word and anything that is not after Christ. Christ is the only way to God, to good things, to good healing, health, deliverance and peace here on earth and after death.

There was a certain rich man, which was
clothed in purple and fine linen, and fared
sumptuously every day: And it came to pass,
that the beggar died, and was carried by the
angels into Abraham's bosom: the rich man also
died, and was buried; And in hell he lift up his

eyes, being in torments, and seeth Abraham
afar off, and Lazarus in his bosom. And he cried
and said, Father Abraham, have mercy on me,
and send Lazarus, that he may dip the tip of his
finger in water, and cool my tongue; for I am
tormented in this flame.

— LUKE 16:19, 22-24

The highest and worse deceit from the devil among unbelievers, church goers and religious people without Christ who also live in sin is prosperity, complete health, all provision without lack and without holiness (Deuteronomy 32:5, 6, 15; Jeremiah 22:21, 22; Revelation 3:14-20). The devil empowered the rich man in the book of Luke with all prosperity, cloth him with purples, fine linen and caused him to fare sumptuously everyday with no single problem. In the gate of the rich man was another person, a poor beggar named Lazarus who doesn't know his right and his place in Christ. With all the authority he had over demons, evil spirits, sickness and famine, he allowed evil spirits to limit him to a beggar, laid at the gate and full of sores. Instead of desiring to break away from the bewitchment and manipulations of the rich man who used his destiny to make much gain, his desires were manipulated to feed from the crumbs which fell from the rich man's table.

And it came to pass, as we went to prayer, a
certain damsel possessed with a spirit of
divination met us, which brought her masters
much gain by soothsaying: And when her
masters saw that the hope of their gains was
gone, they caught Paul and Silas, and drew
them into the marketplace unto the rulers.

— ACTS 16:16, 19

And he saith unto me, the waters which thou
sawest, where the whore sitteth, are peoples,
and multitudes, and nations, and tongues.

— REVELATION 17:15

As a true believer who eventually went to heaven after death, he had the authority from Christ to cast out the spirit of poverty, borrowing, begging and cancerous sores in his body (Mark 16:17, 18; Luke 10:1, 18-20; 9:1; John 14:12-14; Matthew 18:18, 19). He allowed the rich man who probably may be his elder brother, occultic friend, relation or occult grandmaster to bewitch his destiny, sat upon his glory, marriage, prosperity, health and replaced it with wrong desires. Though he was a practicing believer but he was denied of true fellowship with other believers, limited in the gate of the rich man with incurable sickness that sucked his blood little by little

> And I saw the woman drunken with the blood of the saints, and with the blood of the martyrs of Jesus: and when I saw her, I wondered with great admiration.
>
> — REVELATION 17:6

The occult grandmaster fed him with crumbs which fell from his tables and the dogs of the rich man licked his potentials, originals, true destiny through an open incurably sores from the occult world. Through his arrested destiny, star and God's greatness, the occultic rich man fared sumptuously without sickness every day without lack. In addition, his wealth came by bewitching the great destined poor man who became poor to make his enemy rich. Though the poor man eventually made heaven and was carried by the angels into Abraham's bosom because Abraham had extra mansions. What the poor man would have used to build mansions in heaven was bewitched to make the rich man spontaneously wealthy, healthy, popular, great and powerful on earth. The poor man wasted his opportunity, denied many entrances to heaven because his life and potentials was not used for evangelism to win souls, depopulate hell and populate heaven. By God's special grace and mercy, he made heaven narrowly but had nothing in heaven except a place in Abraham's bosom.

> And he cried and said, Father Abraham, have mercy on me, and send Lazarus, that he may dip the tip of his finger in water, and cool my tongue; for I am tormented in this flame. But Abraham said, Son, remember that thou in thy lifetime receivedst thy good things, and likewise Lazarus evil things: but now he is comforted, and thou art tormented. And beside all this, between us and you there is a great gulf fixed: so that they which would pass from hence to you cannot; neither can they pass to us, that would come from thence.
>
> — LUKE 16:24-26

The rich man used his destiny, divine deposits in him which he cultically bewitched to prosper, block heaven's gate for himself, his relatives and uncountable multitudes. He was deceived by the devil, together with all that believed that God must be with him. All his sufferings on earth was gathered by the devil, his occult group and heaped to his end immediately after death. In hell, he lifted his eyes, being in torments and having been used to be served by others, he cried, prayed to be served in hell but his prayers was too late. He asked Abraham for mercy, and the mercy was that Abraham should send Lazarus into hell to continue his service to him as he did on earth. I presume that if not for Abraham's intervention, plus the impossibility of crossing from heaven to hell, the ignorant Lazarus would have agreed. He wanted Lazarus to cross from heaven to hell fire, a place of torments to dip the tip of his finger, just one in water and cool his tongue for he was being tormented in an unquenchable flame. By right, every repented soul, all Christians should not suffer lack of any good thing from the day he gave himself to Christ. Old things should pass away, all things should be made new and the purpose of Christ's death manifests, but remember; there are ghosts in our midst that still fights us.

THREE

THE GHOST'S BATTLE AGAINST BELIEVERS

There is no level you can get on earth in your relationship with God, your position on earth that you will be free from problems or the troubles of this life. The ghost and all the personalities, the angels that left their first estate, their own habitation in heaven doesn't regard, respect anyone or exempt anyone from being attacked when they have the slightest opportunity. And they don't joke with opportunity; that is why they fight had to keep their victims; places captured at all cost. These are the powers that possessed Cain to attack his only brother for offering a holy sacrifice in faith which was respected by God. They attacked Abraham and his wife with barrenness even though they answered God's call, left the idolatrous community and moved out to serve God. These evil forces went into the family of the biological son of Abraham called Isaac and created a problem between his twin boys, Esau and Jacob and made them one of the greatest enemies on this earth. These angels that left their first estate entered into Laban and used him to torment Jacob to serve him for many years without good reward. Joseph was one of the sons of Jacob out of twelves sons that had a great dream but Satan entered into his brethren to envy, jealous, hate him and finally sold him into slavery. In the foreign land, he kept an unbroken relationship with God, a perfect overseer in his place of work and fought against immorality. The devil hated him for living a holy life in the midst of a defiled generation, flamed him up, judged and imprisoned him without been allowed to defend himself.

> And it came to pass after these things, that his master's wife cast her eyes upon Joseph; and she said, Lie with me. But he refused, and said unto his master's wife, Behold, my master wotteth not what is with me in the house, and he hath committed all that he hath to my hand; And Joseph's master took him, and put him into the prison, a place where the king's prisoners were bound: and he was there in the prison.
>
> — GENESIS 39:7-8, 20

When the devil saw that the children of Israel in Egypt were fruitful, increased abundantly, multiplied and waxed exceedingly mighty, Pharaoh became angry and set taskmasters to afflict them with burdens. He made them to serve in rigor, made their lives bitter with hard bondage, in mortar, in brick and all manner of service in the field. He even commanded the Egyptian midwives to kill every male child from Hebrews women upon the stools. When the children of Israel began to cry for deliverance, God appeared, turned their waters, streams, rivers, ponds, pools of water to blood. When the children of Israel cried more to God, He sent frogs into their cities and frog covered all the space in Egypt. There were also lice, many other plagues and when they refused to repent, God sent an angel of death to kill every first born in the land of Egypt, from the first born of Pharaoh that sat on his throne unto the first born of the captive that was in the dungeon. All the first born of cattle and lastly, Pharaoh and his army were drowned by the red sea. If you keep quiet, do nothing, hoping and believing that the evil spirit that possess your home, office, body or any area of your life will stop on its own, you will suffer long and the situation will be worse. If you are fighting but your efforts are not enough, the demons may give you break at times but resume work after. If you only depend on the prayers of others and fail to develop your prayers life to some extent, you will always suffer especially when your prayer contractors are not available to pray for you. If you are praying but you refuse to truly repent, you still have sin, iniquity in your heat, you will not achieve much (Mark 11:25, 26; Matthew 5:23-26). You must not pray against God's reveled will, in unbelief, doubt and contrary to God's word (Psalm 106:13-15; James 1:5-8; Matthew 12:34-37). Fear, doubt, unbelief and discouragement, complaining, shifting blame or getting angry at God without fighting rightly, praying rightly will prolong demonic attacks in your life and home.

Submit yourselves therefore to God. Resist the devil, and he will flee from you.

— JAMES 4:7

Then there was a famine in the days of David three years, year after year; and David enquired of the Lord. And the Lord answered, it is for Saul, and for his bloody house, because he slew the Gibeonites.

— 2 SAMUEL 21:1

After making sure that all sins are confessed and forsaking, you have to rise up in faith and resist the demons. Bind, cast them out and if they resist pour prayers, resist their resistance until they bow. When David was anointed to be the overall King of Israel, he just rushed into the throne and he was confronted by famine. He must have prayed but his prayers were not enough to bind and cast out the level of demon on the throne. He ignored the spirit behind the famine hoping that by righteousness alone and total obedience to the word of God, the famine may just end one day. After the first year, the second, till three years, he went into the prayers of enquiry and God reveled the secrets to him. God didn't find any sin against David but on Saul who was dead at that time. Saul, the King before David was a murderer and the blood he shed was crying in the throne where David was sitting as a king at that time. If there is any demon claiming ownership of your home, any organ of your body, you have to rise up and silence their voice with the crying blood of Jesus.

And to Jesus the mediator of the new covenant, and to the blood of sprinkling, that speaketh better things than that of Abel.

— HEBREWS 12:24

Hast thou commanded the morning since thy days; and caused the dayspring to know his place; That it might take hold of the ends of the earth, that the wicked might be shaken out of it?

— JOB 38:12-13

There are people whose financial foundation, marriage foundation, certificate foundation, every organ of their body and destiny are corrupt, defiled and contaminated. A little amount of money, negative action in the past, invested in your business, marriage, academic or from your ancestors, parents or by yourself may give invitation to a demon. If you defile your marriage vow, treat others unfairly, commit immorality with certain type of people who are badly possessed, your bed will be defiled, polluted and demon may possess your bed. There are people you cheat, take their money wrongly, defraud and you will never be satisfied with money and things money can buy. Billions of people on earth, places you have been to in life, wrong things you did are possessed with many demons. The angels which kept not their first estate, the principalities, powers, rulers of darkness of this world and spiritual wickedness in high places work with demons with diversities of gifts. These billions of demons have different ways of administrations, diversities of operations from the same kingdom. They manifest according to the sins that sinners who cooperate with them committed, according to the strength and the wickedness of the demons involved. Some demons are exposed with more wisdom, knowledge, faith and can counterfeit Christ in healing, miracles and prophecies. Others are schooled, certified and empowered from their kingdom to discern the future, monitor people's activities, speak mysteries, and interpret secrets. Some came from a very hierarchy office with more powers to rule, to dominate, to build strongholds and oppress people with more wickedness than others.

> There was a man in the land of Uz, whose name was Job; and that man was perfect and upright, and one that feared God, and eschewed evil. Now there was a day when the sons of God came to present themselves before the Lord, and Satan came also among them. Then Satan answered the Lord, and said, Doth Job fear God for nought? Hast not thou made an hedge about him, and about his house, and about all that he hath on every side? thou hast blessed the work of his hands, and his substance is increased in the land.
>
> — JOB 1:1, 6, 9, 10

When you have a problem, demons on suicide mission, determined enemy, long time oppressor, grievous problems and any kind of unrepentant situation, don't give up. Don't find fault from God or asking why me. Abel was a righteous person but he mistakenly followed his occultic brother without divine leading. Abraham was called by God, singled out and removed from the company of sinful people to a place that God showed him. While in the will of God, a place that God showed him. The devil attacked him with famine and instead of going to God for solution, he went to Egypt. Esau was hungry, thirsty and in desperate need of food but out of impatience, he sold his birthright. Instead of waiting for the time of God for his dominion, a day set aside by God for his deliverance, he went carnal to fight his brother with hatred.

> And by thy sword shalt thou live, and shalt serve thy brother; and it shall come to pass when thou shalt have the dominion, that thou shalt break his yoke from off thy neck. And Esau hated Jacob because of the blessing wherewith his father blessed him: and Esau said in his heart, the days of mourning for my father are at hand; then will I slay my brother Jacob.
>
> — GENESIS 27:40-41

Isaac told Esau his judgment concerning serving his younger brother and equally assured him of a day ahead, called a day of dominion when his servanthood will come to an end. A day set aside for Esau to have dominion, to break his yoke from his neck but he couldn't wait for that day. He started fighting carnally by hating his brother, planning evil against him because of the blessing that their father blessed Jacob. Esau forgot that there are more blessings to receive from God than from their father Isaac. Jesus our perfect example who for the joy that was set before Him endured the cross, despised every shame, ridicule, insults, ignored every opposition and went to the cross and died for our sins. From every side, He was contradicted by sinners and every blood in Him bled until they were finished, He resisted unto blood, strived against sin and Satan, wrestled against Satan and sin. Therefore, when you are visited by demons, possessed by demons, attack by demons in every part of your body or your house possessed, don't fight carnally. When your ways are blocked, business in trouble, health being devoured, ghost living inside you or in your house with you, don't seek for help in a wrong place. No matter what you are going through, the number of demons living inside your house, your organs and the amount of trouble, deaths grieving you, be strong in the Lord and in the power of his might.

Finally, my brethren, be strong in the Lord, and
in the power of his might. Put on the whole
armour of God, that ye may be able to stand
against the wiles of the devil. For we wrestle not
against flesh and blood, but against
principalities, against powers, against the rulers
of the darkness of this world, against spiritual
wickedness in high places.

— EPHESIANS 6:10-12

Every area of your life may be blocked by satanic stronghold to deny you of your rights, benefits, entitlement, peace, joy and happiness; be strong in the Lord, depend on the power that comes through Him. Don't seek for help from the devil, his agents but from the Lord Jesus, the way, the truth and life. Reject, cast down every evil imagination to seek for help outside Christ or outside his knowledge. Examine your life, check your life, repent of every sin, confess personal sin, sins of your ancestors, ask for forgiveness, for cleansing and deliverance from demonic operations which is the consequences of every sin. Thereafter, begin to pray to God, ask what you want, make your hearts desires, needs known to God. Enter into the supreme court of God in heaven through the prayer of appeal, petition against every demonic judgment that are against you.

> Asshur shall not save us; we will not ride upon horses: neither will we say any more to the work of our hands, Ye are our gods: for in thee the fatherless findeth mercy.
>
> — HOSEA 14:3

> And he said unto them, when ye pray, say, Our Father which art in heaven, Hallowed be thy name. Thy kingdom come. Thy will be done, as in heaven, so in earth.
>
> — LUKE 11:2

> And Hannah answered and said, No, my lord, I am a woman of a sorrowful spirit: I have drunk neither wine nor strong drink, but have poured out my soul before the Lord.
>
> — 1 SAMUEL 1:15

Let your soul's desire to meet God, beseech Him, call on Him, seek his face and pour out your heart to God increase. It is very unfortunate that many praying ministers, deliverance experts, big time senior pastors don't teach their followers the first level of prayers. The first level of prayers of sinners are true repentance, confession of sin, invitation of Christ into their lives and homes. Having done the above, you are now qualified to make your request known to God, expressing your desires (Psalms 42:1-2; 63:1-3; 143:6-9). The next step under level one is to cry to God, supplicate, let Him know one after the other what you are going through (Exodus 22:26; Psalm 34:15, 17; 88:1, 2, 9, 13). In the same level one, utter everything to God, call upon Him, lift up your heart and seek his face through waiting on Him.

> But they that wait upon the Lord shall renew
> their strength; they shall mount up with wings
> as eagles; they shall run, and not be weary; and
> they shall walk, and not faint.
>
> — ISAIAH 40:31

> When thou saidst, seek ye my face; my heart
> said unto thee, Thy face, Lord, will I seek.
>
> — PSALMS 27:8

Under level one prayers, you must forgive your offenders ever before they come to ask for it. You must not break God's word, praying against his revealed will or pray in unbelieve. In that case, you must pray based on the word of God, specifically, confess your faith in the word of God and act according to God's word, no matter the situations oppose to the answers to your prayers. All the contrary situation, negative medical reports, age and words of men and women around Hannah didn't stop her from pouring her heart to God in prayers. You must come to the point that only God can truly save you, deliver you and set you free from every demonic operation (Hosea 14:3). Before you engage in this level of prayers, you must be sure of God's kingdom in you and that his name alone is hallowed in your life. You must be thirsty for God's help, long for his deliverance with undivided mind, asking for mercy. Before you pray against the powers, dark kingdom behind your problem, enemies, you must have reported them to God first. If you are the type that deny others justice, oppress the poor, people under you, you must stop before asking God to stop demonic oppressions against you. If you want God to listen to you, you must listen to the cries of others, the troubled ones, pity them and try to help the helpless, no matter how little. If you want God to stop your troubles, demonic oppressions, stretch your hand of mercy to the poor, the needy, the sufferings and people who are crying for help.

> In that day shall there be an altar to the Lord in the midst of the land of Egypt, and a pillar at the border thereof to the Lord. And it shall be for a sign and for a witness unto the Lord of hosts in the land of Egypt: for they shall cry unto the Lord because of the oppressors, and he shall send them a saviour, and a great one, and he shall deliver them.
>
> — ISAIAH 19:19-20

If you want God to destroy any satanic altar built in your house, homes, body that harbors demons, you must help the helpless, the hopeless around you or look for them if they are not around you. After these levels one prayers with their subheadings, appealing to God and been assured by God's word for justice, then you proceed to level two. In this level two, under the subheading one as a true child of God, a practical Christian, enforce the devil to leave your body, home, office and all your activities here on earth. But even before you start, you are required to prepare very well because this involves confronting demonic stronghold, territories, camp, evil altars under the supervision of principalities. Some of these territories, dark rooms, altars, ancestral shrines are controlled by evil powers, rulers of darkness of this world that are in charge of practicing wicked activities all over the world. Therefore, that you are born again, filled with the Holy Ghost, give your tithes or living a holy life are not enough for them to allow old things to pass away.

Finally, my brethren, be strong in the Lord, and in the power of his might. Put on the whole armour of God, that ye may be able to stand against the wiles of the devil. For we wrestle not against flesh and blood, but against principalities, against powers, against the rulers of the darkness of this world, against spiritual wickedness in high places. Wherefore take unto you the whole armour of God, that ye may be able to withstand in the evil day, and having done all, to stand. Stand therefore, having your loins girt about with truth, and having on the breastplate of righteousness; And your feet shod with the preparation of the gospel of peace; Above all, taking the shield of faith, wherewith ye shall be able to quench all the fiery darts of the wicked. And take the helmet

of salvation, and the sword of the Spirit, which
is the word of God: Praying always with all
prayer and supplication in the Spirit, and
watching thereunto with all perseverance and
supplication for all saints.

— EPHESIANS 6:10-18

Before you enter into this level of prayer warfare, you must put on the belt of truth (Ephesians 6:14; Luke 12:35; 1 Peter 1:13). You must put on the breast plate of righteousness, living a holy life even in the midst of battle, poverty, famine of every good thing (Ephesians 6:14; 1 Peter 1:14-16). Another step of preparation is for you to put the shoes of the gospel of peace (Ephesians 6:15; Romans 1:16, 17). Put on the shield of faith no matter the negativities staring at your face, have faith in your deliverance (Ephesians 6:16; Hebrews 11:32-34; 1 Peter 5:9; 1 John 5:14). Put on the helmet of salvation, keep your relationship with Christ under any circumstance without compromising your faith (Ephesians 6:17; 1 Thessalonians 5:8). And finally, put on the sword of the spirit, study how to use the word of God in battle, prayer warfare (Ephesians 6:17, 18; Matthew 4:1-11; Psalms 119:11; Hebrews 4:12; 1 Peter 3:15).

For though we walk in the flesh, we do not war after the flesh: (For the weapons of our warfare are not carnal, but mighty through God to the pulling down of strong holds;) Casting down imaginations, and every high thing that exalteth itself against the knowledge of God, and bringing into captivity every thought to the obedience of Christ.

— 2 CORINTHIANS 10:3-5

Submit yourselves therefore to God. Resist the devil, and he will flee from you.

— JAMES 4:7

It is after the above level two in subheading one that you enter the last subheading, which is spiritual warfare, pulling down the strongholds. Unfortunately, this is where many prayers against demonic operations starts with many people in deliverance operation. Of a truth, many deliverance ministers may not have all the time to tell you the above. It is better detailed when true believers get involved in Bible studies, personal quiet time, offering yourself to the Lord in consecration (Hebrews 10:25; Mark 1:35; Acts 13:1, 2; Luke 9:28-35; Matthew 26:37-44; Romans 12:1, 2; Hebrews 13:15). It is too bad in Christendom today to say that many professing believers don't know the scriptures and church leaders no longer get committed in deep Bible study. Many are only interested in prophesies, miracles, signs, wonders without deep knowledge of Christ and the word of God.

> And ye shall know the truth, and the truth shall make you free. If the Son therefore shall make you free, ye shall be free indeed.
>
> — JOHN 8:32, 36

Any prophesy, deliverance, miracles, signs, wonders, prosperity, power, anointing, promotion and every good thing here on earth without deep knowledge of God's word will eventually bring victims into more bondage. It increases demonic operations, suffering, hardship and all kinds of problem here or in the world to come after death. That is why it is not good to cast out demons without proper preparations like putting all the amors of God (Matthew 12:43-45; Ephesians 6:10-18). If you cast out demons from anyone, it is important that the person must be followed up through Bible study with brethren, fellowshipping with God and offering himself always in consecration to God. Failure to do so, the cast out demons from a place, body and homes will return with seven other spirits more wicked than himself. The state of the person will be worse than the first and that is why the deliverance in our generation is getting worse by the day. Resisting demons, casting out evil spirit is not the major work but keeping your life out of sin is the most important thing. God may refuse to answer your prayers to cast out demons if He is sure that you will not live above the sin or the sins that invited the demons into your life or home. That is an act of love from God because your live is better with few demons than more seven demons who are more wicked than the one you have now (Matthew 12:43-45).

Shortly before the coming of Christ, not only that houses, homes, properties, farm land, offices and virtually everything was possessed but human bodies were possessed by the angels that left their first estate. On Christ's arrival here on earth, He met multitudes who were demonized and possessed with all manner of sickness and diseases (Matthew 4:23-25). He met many with leprosy, blindness, withered hand, fear, lame, maimed, grieved, dumb, lunatic, barren, unclean, plagued, lie at the point of death, with issue of blood, disabled, deaf, toiled all night, impotent and death. All the above were the activities of the devil when Christ came here on earth and none of the above demonic oppressions survived under Christ. Before He left this world, He wrote a will for his followers, for me and you.

And these signs shall follow them that believe;
In my name shall they cast out devils; they shall
speak with new tongues; They shall take up
serpents; and if they drink any deadly thing, it
shall not hurt them; they shall lay hands on the
sick, and they shall recover.

— MARK 16:17-18

His followers who kept to his word saw a lame man who was lame for forty years in the beautiful gate and commanded him to rise up and walk and he did. They met Aeneas who was paralyzed and healed the diseased leg. They came across Dorcas and Eutychus who was killed by Satan and raised them from dead (Acts 3:1-11; 9:32-43; 20:9-12).

EXAMPLES OF DEMONIC OPPRESSIONS

Our generation needs more help, deliverance and divine intervention from demonic attacks than all the past generation put together. We are living in the last time, last times, later day, last days and the conditions within the Christian profession at this close day are centered around the system of denials. The denials we are experiencing in this generation is denial of sound doctrines, denial of God, denial of authority, denial of Christ's coming, denial of Christ's second coming, denial of Christian living and denial of faith. One, two or more of the denials above can open doors for demonic oppressions and if repentance is delayed, there will be demonization of human body and places that belonged to the victims. At that point, the victims will be attacked by all manner of impossibilities, incurable sickness, diseases, infirmities and plagues. Because of the above denials, many will enter into covenant with the devil and more demons will be released to use them against others.

And Balak said unto him, Come, I pray thee, with me unto another place, from whence thou mayest see them: thou shalt see but the utmost part of them, and shalt not see them all: and curse me them from thence. And he brought him into the field of Zophim, to the top of

Pisgah, and built seven altars, and offered a
bullock and a ram on every altar.

— NUMBERS 23:13-14

Don't forget; Balak the King of Moab were relations of Israel,
yet demons possessed him, his princes and all their leaders to
build twenty-one altars to place a curse upon them. Let me tell
you briefly what Balak, Balaam and all the princes of Moab tried
to do against their innocent relatives; the children of Israel.
What is a curse? A curse is an evil wish or utterance said against
a person or persons. It is an evil word put together to torment a
person or a group. It is like a vehicle of problems driving from
one part of someone's body to another. It is an invisible barrier
to keep a person away from God's plans, promises and
blessings. It is a direct opposite of blessings. It is a spell cast
upon a person to control his life wrongly against God and his
children here on earth.

FOUR

KINDS OF EVIL CURSE

C urse of sudden death, Curse of destruction., Curse of none-achievement, Curse of poverty. Curse of accidents, Curse of hatred and rejection. Curse of infirmity and Curse of spiritual blindness. Curse of mismanagement, Curse of financial misappropriations, Curse of borrowing and begging. Curse of late marriage, Curse of marital disharmony, Curse of mental illness and Curse of suicide.

When you are placed under a curse, what happens?

- All efforts the victim put in life to succeed will fail to yield good result.

- Victim's efforts in life will be resisted by demons involved.

- Such victim may be experiencing abnormal fears each time he/she plans to do anything right.

- Things that will be happening to victims will be strange, mysterious and unnatural.

- Trails will refuse to end as problems will be coming one after the other.

- A victim receives all manner of failure, strange problems and hardships.

- Victims will be having marital failure and all manner of failure in many areas.

- Curses can discover victim's destiny and destroy them.

- Curses can afflict, oppress and waste victim's stars.

- Curses can influence people into wrong decisions

- Curses can capture victim's progress and destroy them.

- Curses can arrest victims promising stars and frustrate their great greatness.

- Curses can mark people with invisible marks of hatred and rejection, anywhere they go in life.

- Curses can close victim's good doors and opportunities permanently.

- Curses can force victims to abandon good relationships, jobs and projects.

- It can manipulate victims to look for help in wrong places where their bondages will increase.

- Curses can promote victim's problems, put them in poverty and lack all their lives.

- Curses bring all manner of marital imbalance, hostility and abuse.

- Curses can destroy victims understanding and cause them to act foolishly.

- It can delay victims from getting married and even stop them from getting married at all.

- It can cause divorce, polygamy, childlessness and other marital problems.

- It can keep victims in touch with only their enemies everywhere they go in life.

- Cursed people experience poor finishing and can be forced to abandon good things half way.

- Some suffer from mysterious problems, strange attacks, health failures and heart-breaking occurrences.

- Unchallenged curse can cleave into the lives of her victim and follow them to the grave.

- Extreme curses are addressed and called by name in deliverance, curses on suicide mission.

- Their trials always refuse to end, they come and go and never leave forever.

- Their brilliant children can suddenly become dullard, disobedient, begin to fail exams and uncontrollable.

- Their riches suddenly perish and they will be left with strange struggling and lack.

- They will be stubborn and unable to take good counsel until they make terrible mistake.

Let me give you just one or two examples out of numerous letters I received almost on daily bases. On June and July 2021 from people who go through demonic oppressions.

THE FIRST LETTER

Hello,

My name is (…) and I would like to get your opinion on a demonic situation I am having.

This demon has been following me for years. Since around 2002 or 2003, I started experiencing some very crazy things sure as something shaking the bed, something trying to get into the bed with me. It would try to come up from the bottom of the bed. Every time I relocated, this thing followed and I have traveled and lived in a few states.

I am going to shorten this story a little bit, but know this thing has followed me doing some crazy stuff since the early 2000s.

I moved to Buffalo NY in 2019, and of course, this thing followed. However, now it's started showing itself. I was living in an apartment when I first moved here and I started seeing a mist or fog moving around the wall. It still did the bed shaking, sometimes it would get under the bed and kick it.

I moved into my house a year ago and at first, it was the same stuff it always did. Then it started manifesting. One night I saw a half of a body, another night, something appeared like a ghost right in front of the sofa I was sleeping on but I know it was a demon, as I don't believe ghost exist. One night I saw something at the bottom of the stairs and then it ran up the stairs. It resembled a ET, but shorter. I could hear it walk and sometimes it bumped into things.

I had a pastor come over and pray authority Prayers but it then went and got some of its friends and came back. Then it attached itself to me. After the first pastor came, I have had other pastors/priest try to remove them (some of them was questionable). I had others tell me about some aura and energy stuff which I tried because I was desperate and of course paid them money for absolutely nothing.

I can see these things at night just floating around the room. They change into different shapes and even insects. They wake me up during the night so I can see their foolishness. I have asked the demons to leave. From what I understand, they are supposed to obey being that I have accepted Jesus as my Lord and Savior. But what do I do when they don't obey?

I have changed my whole life to live for Christ and yet I not anyone else can get the demons to leave. I just know understand. Any suggestions?

I look forward to hearing from you.

THE SECOND LETTER

I just read your book "praying with the blood of Jesus" I plan on having my husband read the prayer from the book for our family. We are experiencing attacks in our life. My husband woke up and saw a demon crawling on top of me last month. I was asleep. There was a woman who cursed people and said she was a witch that lived in our home before we bought it. I need a cleansing prayer for our home I believe. Many people have seen what we believe to be demons in our home. We are Christians. Please give me advice what to do.

We have lived in our house 11 years. We've had strange activity since moving in. Sometimes we smell cigarette smoke strong and no one here smokes. Other times people think they have seen a black shadow. Or feel like they are not alone.

Thank you for your guidance. I have ordered the books you said to order. I will read them as soon as they come in the mail.

Sincerely (…).

MY REPLY

I fully understand what you are saying. Those demons are legally invited to live in that house and may have lived there longer than you can imagine before you start living there. Spiritually, they see you as an intruder and if you are not strong in prayer with good relationship with God they may start engaging, marrying everyone in the house, attacking everyone in the house. And with time everything done by anyone in the house, including health will be brought low (2 Samuel 21:1; 2 Kings 4:1; Jeremiah 16:1-4, 110-12). They can accuse you before God unknown to you, question the source of the money you used in buying the house, how clean and claim that their altars were installed in the household before you came with your prayer altar, calling your God. They will get angry and start attacking you, everyone in the house and all that gives you joy, peace and prosperity. Solution, my books recommended and understand what you are going through better. You, everyone, everything, the house itself need deliverance and it has to be fought spiritually (Ephesians 6:10-18; 2 Corinthians 10:3-5).

SPIRITUAL WARFARE, MY SUGGESTIONS

Before we go into the prayers of decrees, let me make this point clear; the source of sickness and demonic operations is Satan. Though, the causes are many but the principle cause is inherited sinful foundation and direct personal sinful acts.

> So went Satan forth from the presence of the Lord, and smote Job with sore boils from the sole of his foot unto his crown.
>
> — JOB 2:7

> Afterward Jesus findeth him in the temple, and said unto him, Behold, thou art made whole: sin no more, lest a worse thing come unto thee.
>
> — JOHN 5:14

Job was a perfect man, upright with complete fear of God who eschewed evil but yet, Satan smote him with sore boils from the sole of his foot unto the crown. When he saw that Job did not resist him, he went ahead to cause more trouble in his life, family and business. His wife also never resisted the devil but must have cursed God before trying to convince her husband like Eve did to Adam but Job retained his integrity. You may have purity, good relationship with God and man but if you don't know how to resist the devil, you may suffer satanic oppression unto death (Luke 16:19-31). By the power of God's mercy, you can be delivered, healed and set completely free from demonic oppression but if you don't know how to resist the devil when he comes back for another attack, your deliverance can be lost (Matthew 12:43-45). By the time David took over the throne of Israel from King Saul, all his sins had been forgiven, he has clean hands, pure heart and was already delivered from vanity.

> Then there was a famine in the days of David
> three years, year after year; and David enquired
> of the Lord. And the Lord answered, it is for
> Saul, and for his bloody house, because he slew
> the Gibeonites.
>
> —   2 SAMUEL 21:1

Even with clean hands, good relationship with God, famine devastated the nation under his watch because of the sin of his predecessor, the crying blood in the throne. He must have prayed but his prayers were not enough and his knowledge was limited. Let me sound this important warning; if you pray and fail to receive answer; the failure cannot be possible from God's side. Do you know why? God is more willing to answer prayers, to give, to bless, heal, deliver you from satanic oppression and perform miracles for you more than you are willing to ask and receive. You must understand that every problem, demonic oppressions has levels of bondage with specific information on how to dislodge them.

> But other fell into good ground, and brought forth fruit, some an hundredfold, some sixtyfold, some thirtyfold. Who hath ears to hear, let him hear.
>
> — MATTHEW 13:8-9

If your ancestors were idol worshippers, murderers, fetish, diabolic, covenant breakers, who never kept marriage vows, their commitments, promises to others, you must be ready to fight more battles. If at conception, you fell by the wayside, stony places, among the thorns, you must be ready to fight against demons that devour, scorch and choke people's greatness. If your parents are born again, filled with the Holy Ghost power, sanctified and prayerful but you are lazy, prayerless, you will not score high mark, pass mark in spiritual warfare. Look at David's sons, daughter, Eli's children, Moses' children and Ahab's family.

> Seest thou how Ahab humbleth himself before me? because he humbleth himself before me, I will not bring the evil in his days: but in his son's days will I bring the evil upon his house.
>
> — 1 KINGS 21:29

The humility of Ahab, his repentance and prayerfulness kept a whole nation, his family out of war, demonic oppressions, problems, evil all the days of his life on earth. After his death, the devil opened the fill of iniquity closed by his humility, repentance and prayers for three years (1Kings 21:21-29; 2 Kings 9:1-37). Don't forget, the devil is not only the accuser of the old testament saints. He is still the accuser of new testament believers, adversary, father of lies, a liar, rulers of darkness of this world and a murderer.

> Therefore, if any man be in Christ, he is a new creature: old things are passed away; behold, all things are become new.
>
> — 2 CORINTHIANS 5:17

And I heard a loud voice saying in heaven, Now is come salvation, and strength, and the kingdom of our God, and the power of his Christ: for the accuser of our brethren is cast down, which accused them before our God day and night.

— REVELATION 12:10

As a matter of fact, biblically, old things, sin and its consequences should and must pass away, and all things become new immediately we get born again but don't forget; the devil is still around here. He will accuse you, tempt you, try to quote God's word to you, put hunger in you, take you up to the pinnacle of the temple and try to use you instead of God. He may try to influence you to twist the word of God, cause you to tempt God, but you must not cooperate. He may take you up into an exceeding high mountain, developed world, business opportunities, greatness, all the kingdoms of the world and the glory in them. He may promise to give you political power, just for four years, great congregation, multitude followers, office promotion, healing, deliverance from satanic oppressions, great wealth or ordinary visit to a place. The devil can come up with what you need most at all cost, just a false doctrine, worldly pleasures, few years of riches, just one sexual enjoyment, an opportunity to own a car, a house; name it. He may promise you a talent, voice to sing, to praise God in the church, among sinners, make you a great orator, give you power to perform fake miracle, prophesy; just name it (Matthew 4:1-7)

> Again, the devil taketh him up into an exceeding
> high mountain, and sheweth him all the
> kingdoms of the world, and the glory of them;
> And saith unto him, all these things will I give
> thee, if thou wilt fall down and worship me.
> Then saith Jesus unto him, get thee hence,
> Satan: for it is written, thou shalt worship the
> Lord thy God, and him only shalt thou serve.
>
> — MATTHEW 4:8-10

All he demands is for you to commit a single sin, more sin, to bow down to worship him through an image, to worship the true God through a statue, to offer a single sacrifice to an idol, to swear by other gods, to seek for deliverance in the wrong places, to enter into a cult, false place of worship or witchcraft group. When the covenant children of Israel did few of the above, entered into covenant with the queen of heaven (Jeremiah 7:1-34; 44:15-18), God refused to deliver them from satanic oppressions. He mandated Jeremiah to stand in the gate of the LORD'S house, church to call them unto true repentance. When they refuse; God refuse to answer the prayers of Jeremiah on their behalf and left them under satanic oppressions. To some, who repented but refuse to resist the devil, they remained and died under poverty, lack, famine, sickness, diseases and all manner of demonic oppression.

> There was a certain rich man, which was clothed in purple and fine linen, and fared sumptuously every day: And it came to pass, that the beggar died, and was carried by the angels into Abraham's bosom: the rich man also died, and was buried.
>
> — LUKE 16:19, 22

> Submit yourselves therefore to God. Resist the devil, and he will flee from you.
>
> — JAMES 4:7

After settling your sinful foundation as a believer, you need to discover your foundational level, the number of upstairs, decking the devil built in your foundation, how deep your foundation is. Don't ever compare yourself with another person, even persons of the same parents because you don't know your parent's involvement at your conception and other activities after birth. Let me not bother you so much about foundation. I recommend to you my two-parts books, titled, **"Foundation Exposed"**. SPIRITUAL WARFARE: When you get born again, you are recruited into God's army to fight against the old things that the devil may refuse that should not pass away in your life. You are mandated, empowered and equipped with spiritual weapons to put on and fight for your right. That means you have the right access to your peace, rest, joy, happiness, restful days, nights, good relationships and every good thing in this world. Though many have that right but they are not fit because they fail, refuse, ignore, are deceived not to put on the whole armor of God to fight for their right. They are just like the son of a wealthy man, the heir apparent to the throne and his father's wealth but decided to not to go to the bank to sign some papers and claim the wealth and enjoy his rights as enshrined in his fathers will before death.

> But now in Christ Jesus ye who sometimes were far off are made nigh by the blood of Christ. Now therefore ye are no more strangers and foreigners, but fellow citizens with the saints, and of the household of God.
>
> — EPHESIANS 2:13, 19

> And if children, then heirs; heirs of God, and
> joint-heirs with Christ; if so be that we suffer
> with him, that we may be also glorified
> together. He that spared not his own Son, but
> delivered him up for us all, how shall he not with
> him also freely give us all things?
>
> — ROMANS 8:17, 32

As a believer, son of God, new creature, brother to Jesus, temple of God, King, Ambassador for Christ, sheep of the great shepherded and an heir of God, you must not remain under satanic oppression. You need to rise up to resist the devil, fight for your rights and live above every other creature here on earth. There is a war going on between God's children and Satan's agents and that is why Paul likened Christian life to wrestling, fighting and warfare (Ephesians 6:12; 1 Timothy 6:12; 1 Corinthians 9:25-27; 2 Corinthians 10:3-5; 1 Corinthians 15:30-32). As a believer, you have the right of dominion over every creature, therefore, base your faith on the word of God. Ask specifically, confess faith in God's faithfulness. Believe in the word of God, no matter the opposing circumstances, maintain your confession and faith in the written word of God, not just on mere prophesies you are not sure of. If the evil powers refuse to bow, refuse to stop praying and believing God's word until they bow because they don't have greater power than Christ in you. To avoid defeat, even unto death, avoid to give up, avoid fear, doubt, unbelief, discouragement and never allow any situation, pains to cause you to be discouraged. The failure of Job was that he failed woefully on the area of spiritual warfare until God rebuked him and reminded him of his authority over every creature.

> Thou shalt also decree a thing, and it shall be established unto thee: and the light shall shine upon thy ways.
>
> — JOB 22:28

After praying to God, you must move to the next level of prayer which is warfare, passing decrees that will bring light on your ways. As long as darkness stays, light will not come and light can never come without your decree. There is power in spoken word and it is through that, that God created all things and gave us power to follow suit. Instead of passing decrees, Job watched the devil to have his ways in his life, family and the works of his hands. Instead of directing his strength to attack the source of his attacker, the devil; he opened his mouth to curse his day and the devil stood by him to say Amen to his decrees. Instead of commanding, decreeing to the day and the night to cause the devil to perish, he decreed that the day and the night he was born should perish. Instead of filling that day with light, he brought in darkness and asked God to disregard the day he was born (Job 3:1-12). Job cursed the day he was conceived, born, invited darkness, the shadow of death to stain it; he removed the light and asked God to disregard it. He invited the cloud and blackness to live in it and commanded them to terrify it. He even told darkness to seize upon the day, and his night of conception, and death. And commanded it not to be joined unto the months and the year. With Job's authority, he brought in the solitary, killed the voice of joy, cursed his day, darkened his stars, the downing of the day and every good thing. He blamed God, himself, the womb that bare him, the death that spared his live at birth, the breast he sucked and as he was decreeing, the devil stood by to say Amen.

For the earnest expectation of the creature waiteth for the manifestation of the sons of God.

— ROMANS 8:19

And God blessed them, and God said unto them, be fruitful, and multiply, and replenish the earth, and subdue it: and have dominion over the fish of the sea, and over the fowl of the air, and over every living thing that moveth upon the earth. And Adam gave names to all cattle, and to the fowl of the air, and to every beast of the field; but for Adam there was not found an help meet for him.

— GENESIS 1:28; 2:20

In the time of Job's troubles, satanic oppressions, the whole creature were waiting earnestly, ready for battle against his oppressors at his command and decrees but he removed them from the battle field. They waited for his manifestations but he manifested against them instead of his enemy; the devil. His eyes were blinded from seeing his worse enemy who accused him before God for not fearing Him for nothing. He allowed his enemy who accused him and took permission to remove divine hedge about him and his house. He let go off his worse enemy who envied the blessed works of his hands and allowed him, the devil to obtain permission to touch his health and wealth. All the while the devil was speaking to God, Job was not talking, not praying, his children was never thought about warfare. They only knew how to feast from house to house, inviting their brothers and sisters and were never sensitive of the presence of the devil, an enemy in this world. God waited for Job, anyone in his family to challenge the devil, contradict his word but nothing happened until the devil got finished, obtained permission to attack, oppress, gathered the power and left the presence of God. The day the devil attacked the sons and daughters of Job in his absence, they were eating and drinking in their elder brother's house.

And I sought for a man among them, that should make up the hedge, and stand in the gap before me for the land, that I should not destroy it: but I found none.

— EZEKIEL 22:30

So, shall they fear the name of the Lord from the west, and his glory from the rising of the sun. When the enemy shall come in like a flood, the Spirit of the Lord shall lift up a standard against him.

— ISAIAH 59:19

When the prayerless messenger of Job, who was only spared to bring bad news reported, saw what happened, he said it was done by the fire of God from heaven. The other ignorant spared messenger instead of accusing the devil said it was caused by the Chaldeans and another one accused the great wind from the wilderness. When Job heard all the bad news, he fell down to worship God in prayer, which is the first level of prayer. But his failure was the lack of knowledge of warfare, the source of his problems, resisting the devil and believing that it was God's will to take what He gave to him (Job 1:1-20; 2:1-7).

And said, Naked came I out of my mother's womb, and naked shall I return thither: The Lord gave, and the Lord hath taken away; blessed be the name of the Lord. Then said his wife unto him, Dost thou still retain thine integrity? curse God, and die. But he said unto her, Thou speakest as one of the foolish women speaketh. What? shall we receive good at the hand of God, and shall we not receive evil? In all this did not Job sin with his lips. Hast thou commanded the morning since thy days; and caused the dayspring to know his place; That it might take hold of the ends of the earth, that the wicked might be shaken out of it?

— JOB 1:21; 2:9, 10; 38:12, 13

Job maintained good relationship with God but he suffered too much in ignorance by believing that God gives evil and good. Again, instead of ignoring the accusations of the devil through his agents; Job's friends. He started arguing with them, claiming innocent without commanding the morning and other creatures who were eagerly waiting earnestly to fight for him at his command. Instead of decreeing, commanding the light to shine at his darkness on his ways; he moved them out of the battle field of his life and stayed alone with the devil and his helpless friends. Even in his sufferings, poverty, pains, afflictions and demonic oppressions, the morning that comes each day of the battle was waiting for his command. The dayspring was waiting for him to place them rightly and position them to fight for his deliverance. Both the morning, all the days of his battle that sprung up waited in vain for Job's command and decrees. If Job had decreed, commanded them, the creatures, they would have held the end of that particular day that his problem started and shake them out, stop the wicked from operating the next day.

> Then spake Joshua to the Lord in the day when the Lord delivered up the Amorites before the children of Israel, and he said in the sight of Israel, Sun, stand thou still upon Gibeon; and thou, Moon, in the valley of Ajalon. And the sun

stood still, and the moon stayed, until the people
had avenged themselves upon their enemies. Is
not this written in the book of Jasher? So, the
sun stood still in the midst of heaven, and hasted
not to go down about a whole day. And there
was no day like that before it or after it, that the
Lord hearkened unto the voice of a man: for the
Lord fought for Israel.

— JOSHUA 10:12-14

In those days was Hezekiah sick unto death.
And Isaiah the prophet the son of Amoz came
unto him, and said unto him, thus saith the Lord,
set thine house in order: for thou shalt die, and
not live. Then Hezekiah turned his face toward
the wall, and prayed unto the Lord, and said,
remember now, O Lord, I beseech thee, how I
have walked before thee in truth and with a
perfect heart, and have done that which is good
in thy sight. And Hezekiah wept sore. Then
came the word of the Lord to Isaiah, saying, Go,
and say to Hezekiah, thus saith the Lord, the
God of David thy father, I have heard thy
prayer, I have seen thy tears: behold, I will add
unto thy days fifteen years. And I will deliver

thee and this city out of the hand of the king of
Assyria: and I will defend this city.

— ISAIAH 38:1-6

Most Christians are still operating under ignorance, held down
only at the level of asking without seeking and knocking. Moses
stayed with God for forty-days asking, seeking and knocking at
the door and never left until something happened. Joshua and
the elders of Israel knocked at the door of God until Achan was
exposed and the cause of the enemy's oppression revealed.
Hannah refused to leave the temple, knocking, praying and
fasting until God remembered her and destroyed her
barrenness. Elijah fasted and prayed for forty-days and nights
until God answered him. Though a King, Ahab, a sinner fasted,
refused to eat until God suspended the imminent judgment
against his house and the whole nation for three-year till, he
died. Jehoshaphat and all Israel fasted, knocked at the heavenly
door until their prayers shifted their battle out of their reach to
Himself. The Ninevites fasted and God called back heavenly
soldiers assigned to overthrow their city and their prayers
brough national salvation and great revival. Daniel fasted for
twenty-one days and God sent reinforcement from heaven to
help him. Not even lions, evil decrees of kings, conspirators in
his office could stop him from knocking at divine doors. At his
prayers, the locked up of heaven by the devil for seventy-years

was opened and the captive children of Israel under demonic oppression were terminated. And what shall I more say? For time would fail me to tell of Ezra, and of Esther, and of Mordecai, and of Nehemiah, and of the disciples of Jesus Christ; who through prayer, fasting, and decrees subdued demonic kingdoms, obtained great promises, secured personal deliverances, obtain national deliverances. And of Jesus Christ; who wrestled in the cross, overcame sin, Satan, blot out the handwriting of ordinances that was against us, contrary to us, took it out of the way, nailed it to his cross? And spoilt principalities, powers, the rulers of the darkness of this world and spiritual wickedness in high places. He made a show of them openly, triumphed over it and empowered believers to do likewise through the prayers of decrees.

FIVE

WHAT IS A DECREE?

I am going to take the definition from my popular best number one selling book, **35 Special Dangerous Decrees**.

EVIL DECREES

When we speak of decree, we mean a strong and unshakeable utterance, or exercise of power through word and command, which is next to certainty. A decree can also be in form of an order that has equivalent force of law. It can be defined also as a religious ordinance enacted by a council or a particular head. A decree is a way of foreordaining wills. It is like a judgment delivered in a probate court, which confirms an order judicially. Decrees take many forms. There are good decrees, as well as bad and evil decrees. While an evil decree can bring someone under the influence of curses, spells and all manner of evil, good decrees, sometimes rendered forcefully, set people free and brings restoration and serenity. When an evil person says any evil thing and stands firm on it, those words actually become evil decree. An evil decree can destroy or kill. Evil decrees cannot be taken to be simple evil wishes against people; rather they are strong evil utterances or commands said in forceful manners. Evil decrees are evil words put together to torment peoples' lives. They bring invisible barriers that can keep people out of God's programs and promises. Evil decrees frustrate everything their victims do and can bring frustration at the verge of success. It is a decree said to limit a person or persons to certain levels of life. Evil decrees can cause many problems in peoples' lives. They put people under serious bondages. Evil decrees can cause premature deaths. Evil decrees can cause fatal accidents, losses of lives and destroy marriages. An evil decree can bring someone under the power of poverty. An evil decree can stimulate someone to commit suicide and can make people marry at later ages of their lives. Yokes of mental illness can be imposed on people through evil decrees.

Evil decrees initiate uncontrollable desires for immorality. It brings spiritual blindness and makes people to siphon off treasuries. When one is under the influence of evil decree, such a person would not see things rightly. He or she would likely come under the control of errors, taking actions one is not supposed to take. It can also bring depression and feelings of dejection. It could make people to be unreasonably harsh and unteachable. It can cause people to come under the yoke of vagabond spirits. Victims of evil decrees can be manipulated easily. Evil decrees bring all sorts of things that lead to spiritual backwardness. That is why a brilliant student could suddenly become a dullard and begin to fail exams. Evil decrees can bring people under periodical failures. They put people under demonic powers. That is exactly when people become confused in life, suffering from incurable diseases. Evil decrees facilitate sudden disappearance of good things. They can cause a very rich person to become a beggar and remain under an evil mark of poverty, hardship and suffering. Evil decrees pollute peoples' characters.

It is possible for someone under the influence of an evil decree to be deformed in life. In such cases, such people's destinies are buried while they still live. Dangerous decrees can cause you to lose your job in mysteriously circumstances and prevent you from getting other jobs. It can place people under the yoke of barrenness for years and if such evil decrees are not revoked, such victims would stay barren the rest of their lives.

Evil decrees subject people to pains, agony and prolonged sufferings. They cause miscarriages and painful menstruation. Dangerous decrees can shut the doors of true riches. Evil decrees are often the root of extreme hatred and unavoidable divorces. When a child is under the influence of dangerous decree, such a child's behaviors would be strange.

A Christian under the influence of evil decrees cannot enjoy good things for a long time. Such Christians will continue to experience incessant setbacks in every endeavor. This is because evil decrees cause people to fail in all their ventures. People under this influence are hindered to receive true miracles of God. Instead, they remain entangled with wrong people in life, who influence them to make costly mistakes that can destroy their lives. An evil decree can cause destruction in a twinkle of an eye. It can make an industrious or busy person to become lazy and unprofitable suddenly. Evil decrees multiply sorrow, worry and anxiety.

WARFARE SECTION

DECREES AGAINST DEMONIC OPERATIONS

STEP 1

Spirit of the living God, help me to understand exactly what to pray, what to do as I ought to in other to dislodge every demonic spirit in my life, home and office, in the name of Jesus. Let the Spirit of God search me, my house and office to find out the hiding place of demons in my life, home and office and destroy them, in the name of Jesus. Every demonic plan against my life and everyone in my family, be discovered and be destroyed, in the name of Jesus. Holy Spirit of God, arise by your mercy and intercede for me, my family and my loved ones that are under demonic attack, in the name of Jesus. As I pray in tongues, take over me completely and intercede for me according to the will of God, in the name of Jesus

> And the angel of the Lord spake unto Philip,
> saying, Arise, and go toward the south unto the
> way that goeth down from Jerusalem unto
> Gaza, which is desert. And he arose and went:
> and, behold, a man of Ethiopia, an eunuch of
> great authority under Candace queen of the
> Ethiopians, who had the charge of all her
> treasure, and had come to Jerusalem for to
> worship,
>
> — ACTS 8:26-27

> And the angels which kept not their first estate,
> but left their own habitation, he hath reserved
> in everlasting chains under darkness unto the
> judgment of the great day. Likewise, also these
> filthy dreamers defile the flesh, despise
> dominion, and speak evil of dignities.
>
> — JUDE 6, 8

Speak in tongues, pray as long as you can.

STEP 2

Let the mercy of God enter into my life, my home and my place of work for perfect deliverance from demonic operations, in the name of Jesus. Let every enemy of my salvation and my relationship with God in my house and everywhere be exposed and disgraced, in the name of Jesus. Father Lord, empower me to earnestly contend for my faith in Christ against the operations of the devil, in the mighty name of Jesus. Every demonic judgment, condemnation, your judgment is not final; I reverse them now, in the name of Jesus. Let every yoke of ungodliness put upon me by the devil catch fire and burn to ashes, in the name of Jesus. Let every enemy of the grace of God upon my life and ministry fail woefully, in the mighty name of Jesus. Let the angels that failed in heaven and are now on earth to trouble me be frustrated in my life, home and office, in the name of Jesus. Let all the demons that left their first estate in heaven assigned to trouble me be troubled forever out of my life, home and office, in the name of Jesus. Every demon operating in my life, home and office, I bind and cast you out, in the name of Jesus. Let the fire of God burn to ashes every property of the devil in my life, home and office, in the mighty name of Jesus. Blood of Jesus, flow into the foundation of my life, my house and office block, in the name of Jesus.

But while men slept, his enemy came and sowed tares among the wheat, and went his way.

— MATTHEW 13:25

And the Lord said, Because the cry of Sodom and Gomorrah is great, and because their sin is very grievous.

— GENESIS 18:20

Speak in tongues, pray as long as you can.

STEP 3

Let every dark room in my life, home and office receive the light of God and be delivered out of darkness, in the name of Jesus. Let any invisible chain or mark in any area of my life that is pulling me backward break to pieces, in the name of Jesus. I break and loose myself from the lifestyles of Sodom and Gomorrah, in the name of Jesus. Every seed of sin and its consequences in my life, be destroyed by the fire of God, in the name of Jesus.

Now the serpent was more subtill than any beast of the field which the Lord God had made. And he said unto the woman, Yea, hath God said, Ye shall not eat of every tree of the garden? And the woman said unto the serpent, we may eat of the fruit of the trees of the garden: But of the fruit of the tree which is in the midst of the garden, God hath said, Ye shall not eat of it, neither shall ye touch it, lest ye die. And the serpent said unto the woman, Ye shall not surely die: For God doth know that in the day ye eat thereof, then your eyes shall be opened, and ye shall be as gods, knowing good and evil. And when the woman saw that the tree

was good for food, and that it was pleasant to
the eyes, and a tree to be desired to make one
wise, she took of the fruit thereof, and did eat,
and gave also unto her husband with her; and
he did eat.

— GENESIS 3:1-6

Speak in tongues, pray as long as you can.

STEP 4

Any spiritual marriage assigned to destroy me in my sleep, your time is up; I divorce you, in the name of Jesus. Any wrong sexual urge programmed into my life by my spiritual sexual partner through sex in my dream, dry up, in the name of Jesus. Father Lord, deliver me from uncontrollable sexual desire for fornication or adultery assigned to separate me from God and destroy me. Let every yoke of adultery, unclean sexual thoughts, lesbianism or homosexuality living inside me break to pieces, in the name of Jesus. Father Lord, deliver me from every demonic deposit assigned to torment me with uncontrollable sexual urge, in the name of Jesus. Let every satanic dream assigned to defile my flesh, destroy my future and reduce me to an animal be terminated, in the name of Jesus. Any evil personality that breaks into my house, room to have sex with me without divine permission, I bind and cast you out, in the name of Jesus. I command all my spiritual husbands/wives/children and concubines to be frustrated out of my life forever, in the name of Jesus.

I command any demonic conception that took place in my life in the dream to be aborted without delay, in the name of Jesus. Let every yoke of adultery and all manner of sexual abominations in my life be terminated, in the name of Jesus.

Speak in tongues, pray as long as you can.

STEP 5

Any antichrist spirit living in me, my house or office, I bind and cast you out. Any evil spirit that comes to abuse me sexually in my dreams, I cut off from you forever, in the name of Jesus. Let every seed of carnality planted into my life through dreams be uprooted and destroyed forever, in the name of Jesus. Let the spirit of corruption, defilement and pollution in my life be bound and cast out. Any evil covenant and curse I inherited from my foundation, I reject you, in the name of Jesus. Every spirit of deceit, separation and divorce working against my marriage from the demonic world, I bind and cast you out, in the name of Jesus. Let any seed of hatred, rejection, fighting, disagreement and absence of sexual feelings between me and my legally married partner die, in the name of Jesus.

Now the serpent was more subtil than any beast of the field which the Lord God had made. And he said unto the woman, Yea, hath God said, Ye shall not eat of every tree of the garden? And the woman said unto the serpent, we may eat of the fruit of the trees of the garden: But of the fruit of the tree which is in the midst of the garden, God hath said, Ye shall not eat of it, neither shall ye touch it, lest ye die.

And the serpent said unto the woman, Ye shall not surely die: For God doth know that in the day ye eat thereof, then your eyes shall be opened, and ye shall be as gods, knowing good and evil. And when the woman saw that the tree was good for food, and that it was pleasant to the eyes, and a tree to be desired to make one wise, she took of the fruit thereof, and did eat, and gave also unto her husband with her; and he did eat.

— GENESIS 3:1-6

Speak in tongues, pray as long as you can.

STEP 6

I command any sexual serpentine venom injected into my life or my legally married partner to destroy our marriage to dry up, in the name of Jesus. Any serpent, witchcraft animal, evil personality that married me spiritually, I divorce you and cut you to pieces, in the name of Jesus. Let any evil force that has diverted my sexual urge, killed my true nature and injected unnatural affections into my life scatter and be destroyed, in the name of Jesus. Father Lord, restore in me your true nature, pure desires, holy feelings and your image, in the name of Jesus. Every demonic exchange that has taken place in my life in the spirit, and is now manifesting physically, I reverse you, in the name of Jesus. Any demonic spirit using me to devise iniquity against God, I bind and cast you out, in the mighty name of Jesus.

Speak in tongues, pray as long as you can.

STEP 7

Every yoke of elopement dragging me out from my godly relationship into wrong ones, break and loose your hold over my life, in the name of Jesus. Almighty God, deliver me from the yoke of filthy communication, filthy lucre, foolishness, greed, idolatry, immorality, impurity, incest, love of money, lusts and all manner of evil, in the name of Jesus. Let every demonic lust in my eye or flesh, demonic pleasure, polygamy, promiscuity, seduction, prostitution, sex maniac and all manner of sexual perversion be destroyed, in the name of Jesus. Almighty God, deliver me from every uncleanness, unequal yoke, voyeurism, witchcraft demons, wickedness and spiritual manipulations, in the name of Jesus.

> For this cause God gave them up unto vile affections: for even their women did change the natural use into that which is against nature: And likewise also the men, leaving the natural use of the woman, burned in their lust one toward another; men with men working that which is unseemly, and receiving in themselves that recompence of their error which was meet. Being filled with all unrighteousness, fornication, wickedness, covetousness, maliciousness; full of

envy, murder, debate, deceit, malignity; whisperers, Backbiters, haters of God, despiteful, proud, boasters, inventors of evil things, disobedient to parents, Without understanding, covenant breakers, without natural affection, implacable, unmerciful: Who knowing the judgment of God, that they which commit such things are worthy of death, not only do the same, but have pleasure in them that do them.

— ROMANS 1:26, 27, 29-32

Speak in tongues, pray as long as you can.

STEP 8

Every spirit of unrighteousness, disobedience, evil imaginations, demonic exchange, vile affections, reprobate mind and all manner of sexual perversion in my life, I bind and cast you out, in the name of Jesus. I break and loose myself from all my spiritual demonic relatives attacking me in my dreams, in the name of Jesus.

Father Lord, deliver me from every demonic influence feeding me with all manner of evil in my dreams, in the name of Jesus. Any evil power from the waters living inside me, inside my house and in my office, I bind and cast you out, in the mighty name of Jesus. Almighty God, deliver me from the activities from the woman that sits upon many waters, in the name of Jesus. Every evil kingdom that has established an office in my life, home and my place of work, I destroy your kingdom, in the name of Jesus. Almighty God, deliver me from every evil group militating against my destiny, in the name of Jesus.

> And there came one of the seven angels which had the seven vials, and talked with me, saying unto me, Come hither; I will shew unto thee the judgment of the great whore that sitteth upon many waters: With whom the kings of the earth

have committed fornication, and the inhabitants of the earth have been made drunk with the wine of her fornication. So, he carried me away in the spirit into the wilderness: and I saw a woman sit upon a scarlet coloured beast, full of names of blasphemy, having seven heads and ten horns. And the woman was arrayed in purple and scarlet colour, and decked with gold and precious stones and pearls, having a golden cup in her hand full of abominations and filthiness of her fornication: And upon her forehead was a name written, Mystery, Babylon the Great, the Mother of harlots and abominations of the earth. And I saw the woman drunken with the blood of the saints, and with the blood of the martyrs of Jesus: and when I saw her, I wondered with great admiration. And the angel said unto me, wherefore didst thou marvel? I will tell thee the mystery of the woman, and of the beast that carrieth her, which hath the seven heads and ten horns. And he saith unto me, the waters which thou sawest, where the whore sitteth, are peoples, and multitudes, and nations, and tongues.

— REVELATION 17:1-7, 15

Speak in tongues, pray as long as you can.

STEP 9

Any demonic relationship I inherited from my place of birth working against my relationship with God, I break away from you, in the name of Jesus. Almighty God, deliver me from every evil group fighting to destroy God's plan and purpose for my life. Ancient of days, take me away from the presence of evil kingdom, in the mighty name of Jesus. I break and loose myself from the personality in charge of marine kingdom, in the mighty name of Jesus. Any evil agreement with the devil and his agents working against my faith in Christ, I reject you. Blood of Jesus, speak me out of every demonic captivity and influence, in the name of Jesus. Let the backbone of sin, sickness and disease from the kingdom of darkness in my life break to pieces, in the name of Jesus. I reject any evil name that wants to link me up with satanic kingdom, in the name of Jesus. Almighty God, deliver me from the life of blasphemy, evil company and unprofitable pursuits, in the name of Jesus. Heavenly father, deliver me from every satanic attack designed to waste my life here on earth and take me to hell fire, in the name of Jesus. Any evil head or demonic spirit raised against my deliverance, I cut you off, in the mighty name of Jesus. Any invitation given to the devil and his agents into my life, home and office, I withdraw you now, in the name of Jesus.

The word of the Lord came also unto me, saying, thou shalt not take thee a wife, neither shalt thou have sons or daughters in this place. For thus saith the Lord concerning the sons and concerning the daughters that are born in this place, and concerning their mothers that bare them, and concerning their fathers that begat them in this land; They shall die of grievous deaths; they shall not be lamented; neither shall they be buried; but they shall be as dung upon the face of the earth: and they shall be consumed by the sword, and by famine; and their carcases shall be meat for the fowls of heaven, and for the beasts of the earth.

And it shall come to pass, when thou shalt shew this people all these words, and they shall say unto thee, wherefore hath the Lord pronounced all this great evil against us? or what is our iniquity? or what is our sin that we have committed against the Lord our God? Then shalt thou say unto them, Because your fathers have forsaken me, saith the Lord, and have walked after other gods, and have served them, and have worshipped them, and have forsaken me, and have not kept my law; And ye have done worse than your fathers; for, behold, ye walk everyone after the imagination of his evil heart, that they may not hearken unto me.

— JEREMIAH 16:1-4, 10-12

Speak in tongues, pray as long as you can.

STEP 10

I refuse to embark on any evil pursuit that will bring me into bondage, in the mighty name of Jesus. Almighty God, deliver me from the grip of any sin that brought me under satanic bondage, in the name of Jesus. Let every yoke of sin that is dragging me up and down and from one problem to another break to pieces. Let the consequences of my past sins be destroyed by the crying blood of Jesus and set me free from every bondage, in the name of Jesus. I command the powers behind the long-time bondage in my life to break their hold over my life, in the name of Jesus. I command all evil powers living with me in the house to leave immediately by the power in the speaking blood of Jesus. Let the presence of God manifest in my house and everywhere I go to destroy every form of demonic presence, in the name of Jesus. Every satanic attack against any organ of my body, I terminate then by force by the mercy of God, in the name of Jesus. I break and loose myself from the spirit of vagabond and fugitives, in the name of Jesus. Let any evil name controlling my life, home and office be destroyed and be replaced with the name of Jesus, in the name of Jesus.

Speak in tongues, pray as long as you can.

STEP 11

Heavenly father, send your angel from the third heaven to deliver me from every demonic activity. Let any evil program going on in my life, home or office be terminated by God's divine program for my life, in the name of Jesus. Let any demonic conference organized in my life or office against my destiny scatter in shame. Let every Babylonian kingdom established in my life, home, office or anywhere against God's kingdom collapse, in the name of Jesus. Almighty God, deliver me and my household from every kingdom of Babylon militating against us, in the name of Jesus. I separate myself and family from any ongoing abomination anywhere in this world. Any demonic oppression against me assigned to kill me little by little, your time is up; be terminated in shame, in the name of Jesus. Any problem the devil and his agents are using to drink my blood, I cut it off from your reach, in the name of Jesus. Let the mysteries behind the prosperity of the wicked be revealed, in the mighty name of Jesus. Let any yoke of poverty in my life from satanic kingdom break to pieces, in the name of Jesus. Let the glory of God begin to manifest in my life, home and office forever, in the name of Jesus. I reject any sin and everything the devil and his agents are using to sit upon my destiny, health, glory and everything about me, in the name of Jesus. Any evil voice speaking against my God-ordained marriage here on earth, be silenced by the speaking blood of Jesus.

> And I will cast you out of my sight, as I have cast out all your brethren, even the whole seed of Ephraim. Therefore, pray not thou for this people, neither lift up cry nor prayer for them, neither make intercession to me: for I will not hear thee.
> Seest thou not what they do in the cities of Judah and in the streets of Jerusalem? The children gather wood, and the fathers kindle the fire, and the women knead their dough, to make cakes to the queen of heaven, and to pour out drink offerings unto other gods, that they may provoke me to anger.
>
> — JEREMIAH 7:15-18

Speak in tongues, pray as long as you can.

STEP 12

Let every enemy of the word of God, the plans and purposes of God for my life be exposed and destroyed, in the name of Jesus. Any evil personality that has married me and is sitting upon my marriage physically here on earth, I bind and cast you out, in the name of Jesus. Whoever married me spiritually, you are wicked; I break away from such marriage and I divorce you forever, in the name of Jesus. Almighty God, forgive me if I have made a wrong choice and deliver me from its consequences, in the name of Jesus. Every invitation given to the devil and his agents through sin into my marriage, I withdraw such invitations now, in the name of Jesus. I bind and cast out the demons that followed my marriage from both parents, in the mighty name of Jesus. Every demon of death, poverty, fighting, barrenness, miscarriage and sorrow that flowed my marriage, I bind and cast you out, in the name of Jesus. Almighty God, bring back your joy and true love into my marriage with all the blessings attached to marriage. Let all the demonic spirit beings living in the same house with my physical family be expelled by the power of God, in the name of Jesus. Every organ of my body, soul and spirit, I command you to discharge every unclean spirit in you, in the name of Jesus. Let everything in the building where I live and work expel all demonic presence in them, in the name of Jesus. Father Lord, cleanse my body, soul and spirit together with everyone in my family with the blood of Jesus. I command any evil spirit occupying any space in my life, house and office to leave, in the name of Jesus. Heavenly father, take full possession of my life, family members and this house forever, in the name of Jesus. Any evil spirit following me about to torment me, I bind and cast you out, in the name of Jesus. Father Lord, arise by your mercies and deliver every member of my family from all kind of demonic operations, in the name of Jesus. Any spirit of death, destruction, failure and defeat programmed into the lives of members of my family, I bind and cast you out, in the name of Jesus. I break and loose myself from the spirit that destroys people born in my place, in the name of Jesus. Father Lord, move me away from demonic foundation to the foundation of Christ. Let the common problems associated with everyone in my place of birth avoid me forever, in the mighty name of Jesus.

Speak in tongues, pray as long as you can.

STEP 13

Every yoke of grievous deaths in every area of my life, break to pieces and abandon my life, in the name of Jesus. Let any evil voice crying against me from my foundation be silenced by the crying blood of Jesus, in the name of Jesus. Let every mark of failure, defeat, destruction and death in any area of my life be cleansed by the precious blood of Jesus. Let the special sword prepared by the devil and his agents against me slaughter their owners, in the name of Jesus. Father Lord, deliver me from scarcity of every good thing and take me away from the cloud of darkness, in the mighty name of Jesus. Any evil spirit that has entered into me and refused to leave again, your time is up; come out by force, in the name of Jesus. Let every yoke of my ancestors holding me down break and release me. Almighty God, renounce all your pronouncement against me by your mercy and deliver me from every trouble, in the name of Jesus. Any evil utterance ever spoken against me by anyone living or dead, I command you to expire, in the name of Jesus. I break and loose myself from every inherited covenant and curse, in the name of Jesus.

Speak in tongues, pray as long as you can.

STEP 15

Almighty God, deliver me from the problems I put myself unto by your mercy. Heavenly father, help me to break away from every satanic bondage and take me to my place in life, in the name of Jesus. Every sin their consequences that has refused to let me go, your time is up; abandon my life and leave forever, in the name of Jesus. Let any mountain, agents of the devil and problems that insist on destroying me be destroyed immediately. Let the sins and the demons from the graves of my ancestors flee at the sight of me and at the mention of my names, in the name of Jesus. Father Lord, give me your mark of identify that will scare away demons, in the name of Jesus. Let my presence destroy the presence of evil powers and terminate demonic oppressions, in the name of Jesus. I command Satan, sin, evil and every problem of life to avoid me and flee at the mention of my name, in the name of Jesus. Father Lord, cloth me with the garment of freedom, deliverance and prosperity in righteousness, in the name of Jesus. I receive anointing for contagious spread of divine power and deliverance. Let any evil relationship fighting against my relationship with God and my heavenly benefits be broken, in the name of Jesus. Let my activities here on earth destroy every demonic activity anywhere on earth, in the name of Jesus. Father Lord, let my deliverance spread all over the world and remain permanent, in the name of Jesus.

Speak in tongues, pray as long as you can.

STEP 16

I forever break away from the sins, covenants and curses that brought demons into my life, in the mighty name of Jesus. Almighty God, forgive me of every sin that brought me into unholy relationship with the devil, his agents and all manner of satanic oppression. Any stubborn spirit holding me down in bondage, I bind and cast you out, in the name of Jesus. Let anything in this world/life that opposes God and his word in my life receive destruction, in the name of Jesus. Let every yoke of the devil fighting to separate me from God break to pieces, in the mighty name of Jesus.

> Then all the men which knew that their wives had burned incense unto other gods, and all the women that stood by, a great multitude, even all the people that dwelt in the land of Egypt, in Pathros, answered Jeremiah, saying, As for the word that thou hast spoken unto us in the name of the Lord, we will not hearken unto thee. But we will certainly do whatsoever thing goeth forth out of our own mouth, to burn incense unto the queen of heaven, and to pour out drink offerings unto her, as we have done, we, and our fathers, our kings, and our princes, in the

cities of Judah, and in the streets of Jerusalem: for then had we plenty of victuals, and were well, and saw no evil. But since we left off to burn incense to the queen of heaven, and to pour out drink offerings unto her, we have wanted all things, and have been consumed by the sword and by the famine.

— JEREMIAH 44:15-18

Speak in tongues, pray as long as you can.

STEP 17

I break and loose myself from every demonic covenant and their curses, in the mighty name of Jesus. I command demons following me about resulting from the evil covenant I entered into the past, including the ones I inherited to leave my life alone, in the name of Jesus. I bind and cast out any evil spirit living inside me and the ones living inside my house and office. Almighty God, cloth me with divine garment made with the blood of Jesus against demonic operations, in the name of Jesus. Almighty God, bring me back to yourself, free from any demonic influence and satanic operations, in the name of Jesus. Let any evil covenant and curse hindering the manifestations and answers to my prayers break to pieces, in the name of Jesus. Let every enemy of my life of prayer and fasting and the manifestations of God's glory in my life be exposed and disgraced, in the name of Jesus. Any evil sacrifice going on anywhere against me, expire by the sacrifice of Jesus' blood on the cross of Calvary, in the name of Jesus. I break and loose myself from any relationship with the queen of heaven and her likes, in the name of Jesus.

Beware lest any man spoil you through
philosophy and vain deceit, after the tradition

of men, after the rudiments of the world, and not after Christ.

— COLOSSIANS 2:8

Speak in tongues, pray as long as you can.

STEP 18

I withdraw my promises and commitments from any evil altar, evil group and any satanic kingdom, in the mighty name of Jesus. Let any satanic attack going on against me right inside my house during the day or night be terminated, in the name of Jesus. I refuse to meet up with any satanic demand. Almighty God, empower me to obey you to the latter. Any property of the devil in my house and office, I remove you forever and I replace you with the presence of God, in the name of Jesus. I break and loose myself from every demonic doctrine, demonic philosophy, vain deceit, evil traditions and the rudiments of this world that are not of Christ, in the name of Jesus. I return back all my ill-gotten things to their rightful owners and decree against any demonic attack resulting from my sinful pasts. I command all demons attached to my ill-gotten wealth and riches to be cast out, in the name of Jesus. Let the anointing to confront, war, wrestle and fight all demonic appearances fall upon me, in the name of Jesus. I break and loose myself from the consequences of my past sins eating me up with disgraceful sickness, diseases and all manner of poverty, in the name of Jesus. Father Lord, deliver me from demonic desires assigned to keep me under poverty, suffering, hardship and reproach, in the name of Jesus (Luke 16:19-31).

But if ye do not forgive, neither will your Father which is in heaven forgive your trespasses.

— MARK 11:26

Therefore, if thou bring thy gift to the altar, and there rememberest that thy brother hath ought against thee; Leave there thy gift before the altar, and go thy way; first be reconciled to thy brother, and then come and offer thy gift. Agree with thine adversary quickly, whiles thou art in the way with him; lest at any time the adversary deliver thee to the judge, and the judge deliver thee to the officer, and thou be cast into prison. Verily I say unto thee, thou shalt by no means come out thence, till thou hast paid the uttermost farthing.

— MATTHEW 5:23-26

Speak in tongues, pray as long as you can.

STEP 19

Father Lord, empower me to pray with authority, boldness and faith against every demonic operation in my life, in the name of Jesus. Almighty God, deliver me from every sin, idolatry, hypocrisy and iniquities in the heart, in the name of Jesus. I command every sin of unforgiveness, malice, lusts and secret sin to abandon my life, in the name of Jesus. I refuse to pray and confront demons while regarding iniquity in my heart (Mark 11:26; Psalm 66:18-20; Proverbs 1:28-32; 21:13; Isaiah 59:1, 2; Deuteronomy 1:41-45), in the mighty name of Jesus. I withdraw my case file and everything about me from the altars of darkness, in the mighty name of Jesus. I pour the blood of Jesus upon all the cross road altars, monitoring altars, image altars, animal altars, mobile altars, human altars, marine altars and ancestral altars in my house and office, in the name of Jesus. Let any evil altar in my house manipulating my dreams catch fire and burn to ashes, in the name of Jesus.

> And Moses said unto Korah, be thou and all thy company before the Lord, thou, and they, and Aaron, tomorrow: And there came out a fire from the Lord, and consumed the two hundred and fifty men that offered incense.

— NUMBERS 16:16, 35

Speak in tongues, pray as long as you can.

STEP 20

Let any demonic device, bondage, evil habit, limitations, oppression and curses that has refused to let me go be terminated, in the name of Jesus. I break and loose myself from the yoke of collective bondage, family yoke, environmental yoke, yoke of marital failure, business failure, non-achievement and the yoke of impossibilities, in the name of Jesus. I command all the evil spirits manipulating my life to be bound and cast out (Proverbs 30:7, 8; Jeremiah 33:1-3; 1 Kings 19:4), in the name of Jesus.

> Verily I say unto you, Whatsoever ye shall bind on earth shall be bound in heaven: and whatsoever ye shall loose on earth shall be loosed in heaven. Again, I say unto you, that if two of you shall agree on earth as touching anything that they shall ask, it shall be done for them of my Father which is in heaven.
>
> — MATTHEW 18:18-19

> After these things the Lord appointed other seventy also, and sent them two and two before his face into every city and place,

whither he himself would come. And he said unto them, I beheld Satan as lightning fall from heaven. Behold, I give unto you power to tread on serpents and scorpions, and over all the power of the enemy: and nothing shall by any means hurt you. Notwithstanding in this rejoice not, that the spirits are subject unto you; but rather rejoice, because your names are written in heaven.

— LUKE 10:1, 18-20

Any evil spirit under the sun, especially in my house, I bind and cast you out, in the name of Jesus. Let the demons from any source that has refused to let me go be bound and be cast out, in the name of Jesus. Almighty God, empower me to live above every demonic oppression, in the name of Jesus. Blood of Jesus, speak me out of every demonic arrest and torment, in the name of Jesus. Everlasting God, help me to expel every demon living in me, my house and office, in the name of Jesus. Ancient of days, by your power, I command every demonic activity in my life to stop, in the name of Jesus. Every enemy of my freedom and liberty, your time is up; be wasted, in the name of Jesus. I command every organ of my body and every part of my life to be loosed from demonic oppression, in the name of Jesus. I agree with the author of this book, Dr. Prayer Madueke and command every demon in my life, office and house to be cast out, in the name of Jesus. Let my destiny under demonic captivity be delivered without delay, in the mighty name of Jesus. With the authority given to me as a believer in Jesus Christ, I deliver myself, my household and office environment from every demonic presence, in the name of Jesus. I command every demon in my life, house, place of work to surrender and leave now, in the name of Jesus. I command Satan, the head of demons to be disgraced out of my life and from everything that concerns me, in the name of Jesus. Let confusion break out against evil spirits assigned against me to destroy themselves with their own weapons, in the name of Jesus. Every enemy of God's plan and purpose for my life, be exposed and disgraced, in the name of Jesus. I command the whole creature to arise and frustrate every organized darkness against me, in the mighty name of Jesus.

> For the earnest expectation of the creature waiteth for the manifestation of the sons of God.
>
> — ROMANS 8:19

> Hast thou commanded the morning since thy days;

and caused the dayspring to know his place;

That it might take hold of the ends of the earth,

that the wicked might be shaken out of it?

— JOB 38:12-13

Speak in tongues, pray as long as you can.

STEP 21

Every demonic presence in my life, in my house and office, I tread upon you and command you to leave forever, in the name of Jesus. Let the serpents and scorpions in my life, in my house and everywhere I go die without delay, in the name of Jesus. Let everything that represents Satan in my life, in my house and everywhere I go be destroyed completely, in the name of Jesus. I command every organ of my body with every area of my life to arise and defeat every demonic oppression against me, in the name of Jesus. Let any demonic situation hurting my destiny and hindering God's divine program for my life be terminated, in the name of Jesus. Spirit of untimely death killing the onset of good things in my life, your time is up; receive destruction, in the mighty name of Jesus. I manifest before all creatures and command them to arise in anger and destroy every satanic activity against me, my family and my loved ones, in the name of Jesus. Let my efforts in life, the happenings in my life and family result in prosperity, testimonies and divine presence, in the name of Jesus. Let any demonic being, evil relationship, agent of Satan manipulating me sexually to waste my destiny be frustrated unto death, in the name of Jesus. I command every problem in my life to end today and return no more, in the mighty name of Jesus.

Speak in tongues, pray as long as you can.

THANK YOU!

I'd like to use this time to thank you for purchasing my books and helping my ministry and work. Any copy of my book you buy helps to fund my ministry and family, as well as offering much-needed inspiration to keep writing. My family and I are very thankful, and we take your assistance very seriously.

Thank you so much as you spare this precious moment of your time and may God bless you and meet you at every point of your need.

Send me an email on prayermadu@yahoo.com if you need prayers or counsel or you have questions. Better still if you want to be friends with me.

OTHER BOOKS BY PRAYER MADUEKE

1. 100 Days Prayers to Wake Up Your Lazarus

2. 15 Deliverance Steps to Everlasting Life

3. 21/40 Nights of Decrees and Your Enemies Will Surrender

4. 35 Deliverance Steps to Everlasting Rest

5. 35 Special Dangerous Decrees

6. 40 Prayer Giants

7. Alone with God

8. Americans, May I Have Your Attention Please

9. Avoid Academic Defeats

10. Because You Are Living Abroad

11. Biafra of My Dream

12. Breaking Evil Yokes

13. Call to Renew Covenant

14. Command the Morning, Day and Night

15. Community Liberation and Solemn Assembly

16. Comprehensive Deliverance

17. Confront and Conquer Your Enemy

18. Contemporary Politicians' Prayers for Nation Building

19. Crossing the Hurdles

20. Dangerous Decrees to Destroy Your Destroyers (Series)

21. Dealing with Institutional Altars

22. Deliverance by Alpha and Omega

AN INVITATION TO BECOME A MINISTRY PARTNER

In response to several calls from readers of my books on how to collaborate with this ministry, we are grateful to provide our ministry's bank details.

Be assured that our continued prayers for you will be answered according to God's Word, and as you remain faithful by sowing seeds of faith, God will never forget your labors of love in Christ Jesus.

Send your Seeds to:

In Nigeria & Africa

Bank Name: **Access Bank**

Account Name: **Prayer Emancipation Missions**

Account Number: **0692638220**

In the United States & the rest of the World

Bank Name: **Bank of America**

Account Name: **Roseline C. Madueke**

Account Number: **483079070578**

You can also visit the donation page on my website to donate online: www.madueke.com/donate.

Made in the USA
Coppell, TX
12 October 2021